American History

KNOW-THE-FACTS REVIEW GAME

100 Must-Know Facts in a Q&A Game Format to Help Kids
Really Remember Standards-Based Social Studies Information

by Diana Abitz

NEW YORK • TORONTO • LONDON • AUCKLAND • SYDNEY   **Teaching**
MEXICO CITY • NEW DELHI • HONG KONG • BUENOS AIRES   *Resources*

Cover design by Jason Robinson
Interior design by Grafica
Cover and interior illustrations by Doug Jones

ISBN 0-439-37434-0

1 2 3 4 5 6 7 8 9 10   40   12 11 10 09 08 07 06 05

CONTENTS

Reproducibles

Punch-Out Cards

INTRODUCTION

Welcome to American History Know-the-Facts Review Game!

The *American History Know-the-Facts Review Game* is an interactive, curriculum-based game that encourages critical thinking and can be played in several different ways depending on the number of players and the depth of play desired.

The questions in this book, which are inspired by information found in classroom textbooks for grades 5–8, have been carefully created to entice students to sharpen their knowledge of American history. How students answer the questions and show their understanding of the material will give clues about their proficiency and allow you to use your findings as a standards-based curriculum assessment tool. You can also use the questions to introduce, review, or reinforce a particular topic area.

The questions cover the American history curriculum from roughly the early explorations of the 1400s to the end of the 1800s. They are written in a way that provides a framework and context for the question to help students see more of the complete picture surrounding the historical facts. Because a small package of information can be remembered better by association than by providing just a simple question and answer, some questions contain background information or additional facts to help with the internalization process of learning and remembering. Answers are often explained or expanded to reinforce their meaning and support scaffolding of knowledge.

There are multiple-choice, true-or-false, and single-answer questions. You can decide whether to give the choices for the multiple choice, depending on the skill level of the players or whether students may need hints to answer the question. There are also reward cards that add an element of luck to the game.

The game rules ensure the game's fun factor and were designed to encourage teamwork, inspire cooperation, and give players a sense of participation and accomplishment.

This *Know-the-Facts Game* brings American History to life in an exciting and challenging way. This game will prove to be a delightful learning experience. For all who play—have fun!

What's Inside

- A Know-the-Facts Review Game Board (page 17) with a set of 100 punch-out Game Cards (pages 23–45); 11 Reward Cards, 2 Penalty Cards, and 4 Wild Cards (pages 45 and 47); and Scorecards (pages 19 and 21).

- A reproducible time line (page 11), U.S. Outline Map (page 12), Game Board (page 13), and Scorecards (page 14).

- A reproducible card template you and students can use to customize Game Cards, Reward Cards, Wild Cards, and Penalty Cards (page 15).

- Directions for playing in large- and small-group settings (pages 8 and 9), plus variations for adjusting and adapting play to instructional needs.

Categories

The question cards are divided into seven categories. Each category is identified in the upper-left corner of the card. You can choose questions from one category only and present the questions as a group, or for more of a challenge, mix and match questions from several or all of the categories and present them at random.

- **Exploration**
- **Colonial**
- **Revolutionary War**
- **Early Nation**
- **Civil War**
- **Westward Expansion**
- **Immigration**

Tips for Using the Cards Alone: With seven different question categories, you can select question cards to introduce or highlight material in a corresponding unit of study or to bridge one section of the curriculum to another. You can also pre-select cards for students to use as extra-credit activities, as time-fillers between lessons, or as springboards to further research.

Meeting the Standards

The questions address aspects of the following standards:

Mid-continent Research for Education and Learning (McREL) Standards for U.S. History including

- Era 2: Colonization and Settlement (3 and 4)
- Era 3: Revolution and the New Nation (6, 7, and 8)
- Era 4: Expansion and Reform (9 and 10)
- Era 5: Civil War and Reconstruction (13 and 14)

National Council for the Social Studies (NCSS) Thematic Strands in Social Studies including

- Culture
- Time, Continuity, and Change
- Individuals, Groups, and Institutions
- Power, Authority, and Governance

For more information regarding these thematic strands visit the NCSS Web site at www.socialstudies.org.

Setting Up

To prepare, follow these steps.

1. Punch out the game board, score cards, and question cards by tearing gently around the perforated edges until each comes loose.

2. Laminate for added durability.

3. To make extra question or reward cards, photocopy the front and back of the question-card template (pages 15 and 16) on card stock. Then fill in the cards with needed questions. (Cut out and laminate for durability.) You can also create a new game board and set of score cards, as necessary (pages 13 and 14).

4. Gather other materials needed to play the game including

   • paper and pencils for each team

   • dry-erase markers (if using laminated game components)

   • reference books

   • a time-keeping device (such as a sand timer or watch with a second hand)

5. Store game materials in a small box or resealable plastic bag.

Build student anticipation by talking up the event ahead of time. If it works within your schedule, designating a time on a weekly, biweekly, or monthly basis will help keep a momentum going and give students something to look forward to. Then, select your questions.

Set aside a block of time to play the game. Plan for a 45-minute session the first time the game is played to allow time for going over the instructions. After that, if possible, allow up to 30 minutes to play the game.

How to Play

This game may be played in a whole-group or small-group setting.

Determining Point Value: If the category is Immigration, for example, and no question in that category has been answered correctly yet, the question is worth 100 points. Check off the space on the game board after the question is answered correctly. The next time an Immigration card is chosen, the question's point value is 200, and so on.

Reward Cards and Wild Cards: Reward Cards and Wild Cards are provided to spice up the game. You can make your own using the blank-card template. Follow the instructions found on each card. For team play, however Reward Cards that allow students to consult a resource may only be used for the next question. A Wild Card means the next question can be answered only by the team with the fastest hand-raiser. If that team answers correctly, it receive the points. However, if that team gets the wrong answer it forfeits the same number of points. (If that team had no points, nothing is forfeited.) Before reading the answer, open the floor to another team.

Large-Group (in teams)

The Object: The members of each team work collectively to answer questions correctly in order to earn the highest number of points during a timed game.

Getting Started

1. Divide the class into groups of four students. Ask them to choose a team name related to American history (for example, the Forty-niners).

2. Pass out a scorecard to each team.

3. Review each job listed below and give the teams about 20 seconds to decide who will perform the duties. Having a job for each player increases student incentive to participate.

> **The writer** records the answer on a piece of paper and reads it out loud when necessary.

> **The decision-maker** decides the team's final answer, should there be indecision.

> **The hand-raiser** tries to raise his or her hand first when a Wild Card is in play. The team with the first hand in the air gets to answer first. (The instructor decides which team answers first, should there be confusion.)

> **The scorekeeper** keeps track of the team's earned points.

Note: If there are fewer than four players per team, double up on the duties. If there are more, the remaining players make up the **core think-tank***. In reality, all team members can participate in answering the questions. These core thinkers need to think fast in Wild Card situations.*

Playing the Game

1. The instructor (or another designated **question-reader/timekeeper**) selects a card and reads it to the players.

2. After a short, *quiet* discussion (about 15–20 seconds) within each team, the decision-maker determines the answer and the writer records it on a piece of paper.

3. The writer in each team reads the team's answer out loud.

4. The instructor reads the correct answer on the card to the class. (Remind students not to talk until the complete answer has been read so they don't miss any information.)

5. Each team that answers correctly can have its scorekeeper add the question's point value to the running tally kept on its scorecard.

6. The game continues until all of the spaces on the game board are checked off or the designated game time runs out, whichever comes first.

7. The scorekeeper on each team totals his or her own team's points. The team with the highest score wins. As an incentive, consider presenting the winning team with a small reward. You may allow its members to be the first dismissed for lunch. Or, you may give the winning team extra-credit points.

Small-Group (2–4 players)

The Object: Individual players answer questions correctly in order to earn the highest number of points during a timed game.

Getting Started

1. Reward Cards and Penalty Cards remain in the deck, but remove any Wild Cards.

2. Pass out a scorecard to each player.

3. To determine which player answers a question first, think of a word. Ask the players to guess which letter the word starts with. Whoever is closest goes first. The play continues clockwise.

Playing the Game

1. One player answers a question read by the player to his or her right. (After the first play, the player who just answered a question reads a question to the next player, and so on.)

2. If the player answers the question correctly, he or she can add the question's point value to the running tally on his or her scorecard. If the player answers incorrectly, the answer is read aloud and the game resumes.

3. Play continues until all of the spaces on the game board are checked off or the designated game time runs out, whichever comes first.

Variations

- If game time is limited, load the top of the deck with the most pertinent questions.

- If time allows, and students are ready for an extra challenge, eliminate multiple-choice options when asking questions.

- For small-group play, choose one player to be both the question-reader and timekeeper (see page 7). Pass out a scorecard to each remaining player. Then insert the Wild Cards back into the deck. Explain that all players get the same chance to answer and earn points.

- For small-group play, simplify scorekeeping. Each time a player answers a question correctly he or she collects the card. At the end of the game, the player with the most cards wins.

- Customize the game. Fill out the blank cards with questions based on your curriculum.

- Increase visual literacy by adding pictures to blank cards (famous portraits and so on).

- Have students write their own questions on the blank cards. Then use the questions when you play.

Additional Resources

Tips for Using the Resource Pages
- American History Time Line (page 11)
- U.S. Outline Map (page 12)

Interacting with the resource pages helps students increase their knowledge of American history. Reproduce copies of the pages as necessary and try some of the activity ideas below.

- As a springboard to a whole-class activity, ask students to review the time line. Direct students to research and find at least three interesting facts to add to their own time line. Then, using a long sheet of bulletin board paper attached to a wall, invite students to add their information to the class time line. You may ask each student to find a fact related to another country to add to the time line as a way for students to view their own history in relation to the history of the world. Students can use a different colored marker for these facts and add a color-coded key.

- Students can research and add important people and related information to their individual time line. Or, for the class time line, encourage students to use index cards to record the person's name, the dates he or she lived, and any other interesting information. Then, attach the cards to the time line using yarn or string.

- To enrich the individual or class time line and help increase visual literacy, students can find or illustrate related images and add them to the display.

- When asking a question from one of the question cards, direct students to their outline map. They can visually represent various details of the questions and their answers on their maps.

- Encourage students to research and label on the modern-day political map the geographic boundaries of the United States during different eras. Placing the set of maps side by side allows students to see more clearly how the United States has changed over time.

- Ask students to label the routes people have used to move within the United States during various eras. For example, you might ask students to label the journey of Lewis and Clark, the Oregon Trail, Transcontinental Railroad, Trail of Tears, or Underground Railroad.

Book Links
- *American Revolution Battles and Leaders* by Aaron R. Murray (Dorling Kindersley, 2004)
- *Civil War Battles and Leaders* by Aaron R. Murray (Dorling Kindersley, 2004)
- *Daily Life in the Pilgrim Colony, 1636* by Paul Erickson (Houghton Mifflin, 2001)
- **Dear America/My Name Is America Series** (Scholastic) The books in this historical fiction series are written in the style of diaries and span the eras of American history.
- *Off the Map: The Journals of Lewis and Clark* by Peter and Connie Roop (Walker & Company, 1998)
- *We Shall Not Be Moved: The Women's Factory Strike of 1909* by Joan Dash (Scholastic, 1997)

Web Links
Gold Rush! California's Untold Stories
http://www.museumca.org/goldrush/
From the Oakland Museum of California, this site helps bring to life the world of the "forty-niners." It also includes a impressive array of images.

Immigration: Ellis Island History
http://library.thinkquest.org/20619/Eihist.html
The site provides a glimpse into the immigrant experience at Ellis Island.

Journey Into History: Voyage on the Mayflower
http://teacher.scholastic.com/thanksgiving/mayflower/index.htm
On this site, students can interact with a diagram of the ship and "meet" some of the passengers and crew.

Liberty! The American Revolution
http://www.pbs.org/ktca/liberty/
In the Chronicles of the Revolution, students can read more about important events in the American Revolution. The site also includes an interactive game.

American History Time Line

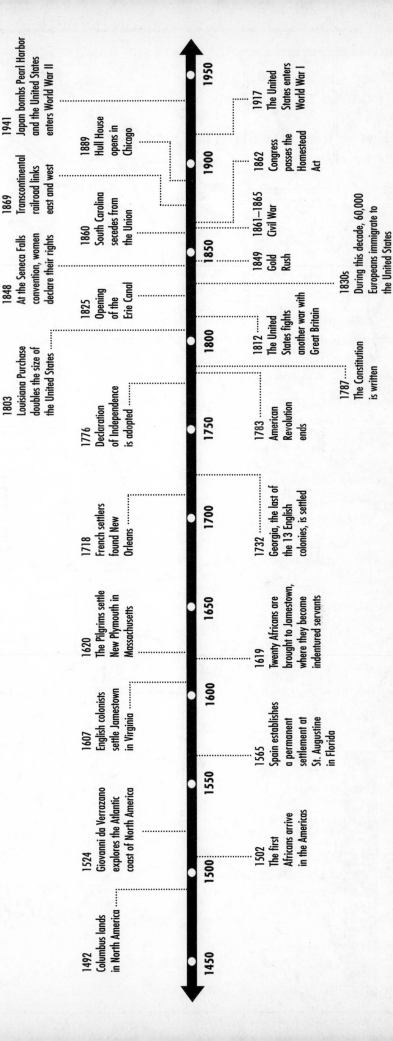

1492 Columbus lands in North America

1502 The first Africans arrive in the Americas

1524 Giovanni da Verrazano explores the Atlantic coast of North America

1565 Spain establishes a permanent settlement at St. Augustine in Florida

1607 English colonists settle Jamestown in Virginia

1619 Twenty Africans are brought to Jamestown, where they become indentured servants

1620 The Pilgrims settle New Plymouth in Massachusetts

1718 French settlers found New Orleans

1732 Georgia, the last of the 13 English colonies, is settled

1776 Declaration of Independence is adopted

1783 American Revolution ends

1787 The Constitution is written

1803 Louisiana Purchase doubles the size of the United States

1812 The United States fights another war with Great Britain

1825 Opening of the Erie Canal

1830s During this decade, 60,000 Europeans immigrate to the United States

1848 At the Seneca Falls convention, women declare their rights

1849 Gold Rush

1860 South Carolina secedes from the Union

1861–1865 Civil War

1862 Congress passes the Homestead Act

1869 Transcontinental railroad links east and west

1889 Hull House opens in Chicago

1917 The United States enters World War I

1941 Japan bombs Pearl Harbor and the United States enters World War II

1450 1500 1550 1600 1650 1700 1750 1800 1850 1900 1950

United States

AMERICAN HISTORY

KNOW-THE-FACTS REVIEW GAME

Exploration	Colonial	Revolutionary War	Early Nation	Civil War	Westward Expansion	Immigration
100	100	100	100	100	100	100
200	200	200	200	200	200	200
300	300	300	300	300	300	300
400	400	400	400	400	400	400
500	500	500	500	500	500	500

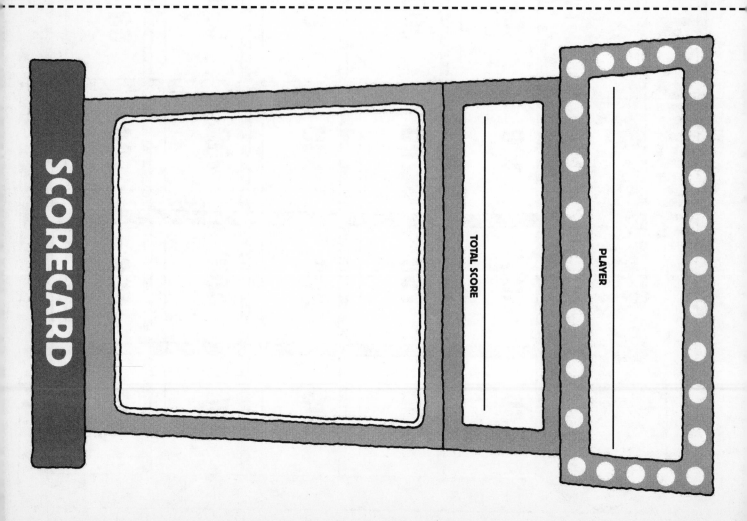

SCORECARD

PLAYER

TOTAL SCORE

SCORECARD

PLAYER

TOTAL SCORE

AMERICAN HISTORY

AMERICAN HISTORY

AMERICAN HISTORY

AMERICAN HISTORY

AMERICAN HISTORY

AMERICAN HISTORY

AMERICAN HISTORY

AMERICAN HISTORY

AMERICAN HISTORY

AMERICAN HISTORY

KNOW-THE-FACTS REVIEW GAME

Exploration	Colonial	Revolutionary War	Early Nation	Civil War	Westward Expansion	Immigration
100	100	100	100	100	100	100
200	200	200	200	200	200	200
300	300	300	300	300	300	300
400	400	400	400	400	400	400
500	500	500	500	500	500	500

PLAYER

TOTAL SCORE

SCORECARD

PLAYER

TOTAL SCORE

SCORECARD

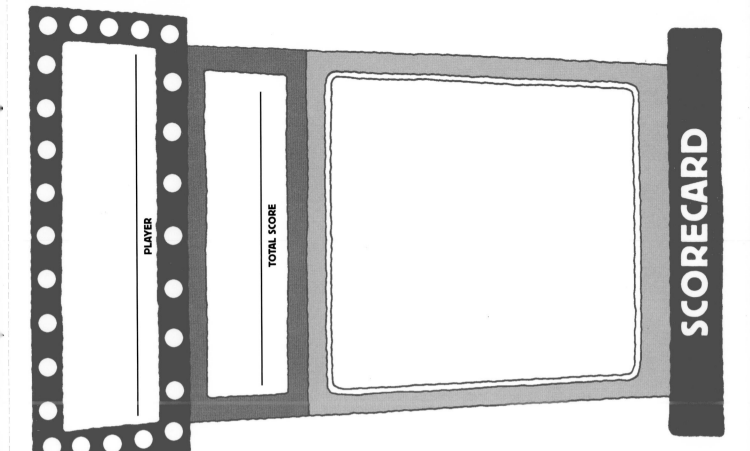

PLAYER

TOTAL SCORE

SCORECARD

PLAYER

TOTAL SCORE

SCORECARD

Exploration

On October 12, 1492, three small Spanish ships landed near an island in the Bahamas occupied by the Taino people. Who was the sea captain of this expedition and what were they looking for?

a. Leif Ericson was looking for a new settlement.
b. Ferdinand Magellan was looking for a new trade route.
c. Christopher Columbus was looking for a new trade route.
d. Captain Hook was looking for gold.

The Spanish government sponsored **Christopher Columbus,** an Italian seaman, to **search for a new trading route** to Asia. (c)

Exploration

On Christopher Columbus's second expedition to the Americas, 17 ships brought adventurous people, food, and supplies to establish La Isabella, a Spanish colony on the island that is now the Dominican Republic and Haiti. What do historians call the movement of people, plants, animals, and germs across the Atlantic Ocean?

a. The Columbian Exchange
b. The Germanic Exchange
c. The American Exchange
d. King Ferdinand's Exchange

Columbus's name was often used for events that occurred in the Americas around his time. **The Columbian Exchange.** (a)

Exploration

How did the Columbian Exchange affect life around the world?

a. New foods exchanged between continents improved food supplies in Europe.
b. Europeans unknowingly exchanged diseases and germs.
c. The population of five continents increased more rapidly.
d. All of the above.

Exchanging crops improved food supplies, which helped to increase populations but unknowingly caused health concerns in the Americas. **All of the above. (d)**

Exploration

Within 30 years after Columbus's first meeting with the Taino people, Spain claimed most of the islands in the Caribbean Sea and much of present day Mexico. What were the ambitious warriors called who conquered new lands for Spain?

a. Explorers
b. Los Hombres
c. Los Combatiente
d. Conquistadors

Spanish soldiers who were primarily looking for gold and new land for Spain were called **Conquistadors. (d)**

Exploration

Hernando Cortés, a 19 year old from Spain, came to Cuba in the early 1500s when the Cuban governor asked him to lead a gold expedition into Mexico. With the help of soldiers and Indians they looked for gold while conquering the Aztecs in what is now called Mexico City. What did they call Spain's newly conquered territories?

a. New Spain
b. New Mexico
c. Americas
d. Yucatan

They called their new territories **New Spain.** It included many of the Caribbean islands, Central America, Mexico, lands now in the southwest United States, and Florida. (a)

Exploration

In 1514 Bartolomé de Las Casas, a Spanish priest and advocate for Indian rights, gave up his land in Mexico to be the "Protector of the Indians." Because Indians were working from dawn to dusk on the land, he persuaded the King of Spain to do what?

a. Have landowners pay Indians for their work
b. Free the Indians
c. Move the Indians to another location
d. Bring in African servants

The King passed the "New Laws of 1542," which said the **Indians would need to be paid for their work.** In response, landowners enslaved Africans to work in the mines and fields. (a)

Exploration

The Spanish founded the oldest European settlement in the United States in 1565 to protect their Atlantic sea routes from England and their land from the French. What is the name of this Florida town that was founded 42 years before Jamestown, Virginia, and 55 years before the Pilgrims arrived at Plymouth Rock?

a. Miami
b. Jacksonville
c. St. Augustine
d. Orlando

Spain's first settlement in the United States was **St. Augustine, Florida. (c)**

Exploration

In 1607 the Dutch explorer Henry Hudson began searching for what?

a. A site to drill for oil
b. The Northwest Passage
c. A ship carrying gold from Mexico
d. All of the above

The **Northwest Passage** was thought to be a water route from North America to Asia. While searching for this passage he initiated trade between the Delaware Nation and the Dutch. He explored a river that was later renamed after him, the Hudson River. (b)

Exploration

In 1673 Father Jacques Marquette and mapmaker Louis Jolliet thought the river Native Americans called the "mighty river" would lead them to the Northwest Passage. What is the name of the river they navigated?

Instead of the Northwest Passage they found the **Mississippi River** and turned back when they realized it headed south, and not toward Asia.

**AMERICAN
HISTORY**

**AMERICAN
HISTORY**

**AMERICAN
HISTORY**

**AMERICAN
HISTORY**

**AMERICAN
HISTORY**

**AMERICAN
HISTORY**

**AMERICAN
HISTORY**

**AMERICAN
HISTORY**

**AMERICAN
HISTORY**

Exploration

In the 1680s the Spanish built settlements in what is today Texas. These settlements were built in this territory to do what?

a. They wanted to keep the French explorers and traders out of the area.
b. They needed to house their conquistadors as they searched for gold.
c. They wanted to show off their architecture.
d. They provided food and shelter for their army and travelers.

The settlements helped to **keep the French out of New Spain. (a)**

Exploration

What current-day state was the last of New Spain's land to be settled by the Spanish?

Cities in the Southwest that originated as Spanish settlements in **California** are San Diego, Los Angeles, and San Francisco. Other cities that originated as Spanish settlements include Santa Fe and Albuquerque (New Mexico), San Antonio and El Paso (Texas), and Tucson (Arizona).

Exploration

A navigator and explorer, Samuel de Champlain founded the trading post called Quebec on the St. Lawrence River in 1608. What country founded the settlements of St. Louis, Detroit, and Chicago during the late 1600s and early 1700s?

France originated these cities as fur trading posts. The rivers near these settlements carried furs bought from the Native Americans out of the wilderness to shipping ports.

Exploration

In 1682 with the help of the Quapaw Indians, Robert Cavelier, sieur de La Salle set out to explore the Mississippi River. What did this Frenchman name the Mississippi River Valley?

Robert Cavelier, sieur de La Salle named the Mississippi River Valley for France by calling it **Louisiana** after King Louis XIV.

Colonial

Spain claimed most of North and South America until the English formed a settlement on Roanoke Island off the coast of North Carolina in 1587. When John White, the governor of Roanoke, left for England to get additional supplies, he was delayed in returning because the English needed their ships and seamen to fight a war with what country?

Spain's King Philip II was unhappy about the English attacking Spanish ships and colonies, so he sent the Spanish Armada to England forcing British ships into battle.

Colonial

When King James I granted a charter to the Virginia Company, it came nearly 20 years after England's failed attempt at creating a settlement on Roanoke Island. Where was the first **permanent** English colony in America?

a. Plymouth
b. Jamestown
c. Williamsburg
d. Boston

The first permanent colony in America founded in 1607 was **Jamestown.** It was named after King James I. **(b)**

Colonial

In 1607 Jamestown was a swampy area filled with mosquitoes that spread disease. Half of the men and boys who settled there died. The other half weren't willing to work. Who was the captain who stopped aristocratic colonists not used to manual labor from searching for gold and forced the colonists to build houses, plant crops, and raise livestock to survive?

Captain John Smith brought order to the colony by enforcing the policy: "He that will not work, shall not eat." His policies made Smith unpopular but helped keep the colonists alive.

Colonial

The Dutch colonists were Protestants who settled along the Hudson River in 1609. Henry Hudson claimed the area for the Netherlands. This thriving trading center, called New Amsterdam, was later renamed after England's King Charles II gave it to his brother. What did they rename New Amsterdam?

The colony was renamed **New York** after the King's brother the Duke of York.

Colonial

When John Rolfe married Chief Powhatan's daughter Pocahontas in 1614, it helped keep peace between Powhatan's people and the Jamestown settlers in Virginia. Where did Pocahontas die?

a. In Jamestown
b. On their plantation in Virginia
c. In London
d. On the reservation

When Pocahontas married John Rolfe, she took the name Rebecca. Two years after they married they moved to **England,** where she died suddenly. John Rolfe and his son Thomas later returned to their Virginia plantation. **(c)**

AMERICAN HISTORY

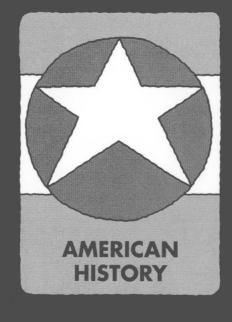

AMERICAN HISTORY

AMERICAN HISTORY

AMERICAN HISTORY

AMERICAN HISTORY

AMERICAN HISTORY

AMERICAN HISTORY

AMERICAN HISTORY

AMERICAN HISTORY

Colonial

What was the role of the first Africans brought to Jamestown in 1619?

a. They were slaves.
b. They were free after they worked for several years as indentured servants.
c. They were slaves until their master died.
d. They were considered equals to the colonists.

Indentured servants were free after working 5–7 years. By 1661 the need for inexpensive labor increased and Africans brought to Jamestown were treated as slaves. **(b)**

Colonial

Why did the Puritans, Quakers, and Catholics leave England to settle in America?

They left to **practice their religious beliefs freely.** Other people came to the colonies in hoping to become wealthy or to seek a better life.

Colonial

The Virginia House of Burgesses met for the first time in a small Jamestown church in 1619. What was the significance of the House of Burgesses?

a. Colonists first utilized buildings for multiple uses.
b. Colonists opened their first store for trade and to sell goods.
c. Colonists took one of their first steps toward governing themselves.
d. All of the above.

Colonists took one of their first steps toward governing themselves when they met as the Virginia House of Burgesses. Designed to meet the needs of the colonists who lived in Virginia, it helped the colony pass laws, collect taxes, and more. **(c)**

Colonial

Before the Pilgrims set foot on land they wrote and signed the **Mayflower Compact.** What was this document?

The Mayflower Compact was an **agreement** to follow rules and laws the colonists thought were just and fair.

Colonial

Which English settlement came first?

a. Plymouth in Cape Cod, Massachusetts
b. Jamestown, Virginia
c. William Penn's Quaker colony in Philadelphia, Pennsylvania
d. The Williamsburg, Virginia, settlement

The first permanent English colony was **Jamestown** in 1607. Women and Africans arrived at the Jamestown settlement one year before the Pilgrims arrived in Plymouth. Jamestown was founded 13 years **before Plymouth.** **(b)**

Colonial

In 1620 King James I of England allowed the Pilgrims to settle in Plymouth so that they could practice their Protestant religion. Merchants in London agreed to pay for the Pilgrims' voyage to America on the Mayflower, in return for what?

a. Half of their profits
b. Gold
c. Tobacco
d. A promise they get out of town for good

The merchants wanted the Pilgrims to send back **half the profits** from their business ventures. **(a)**

Colonial

These Native Americans helped the Pilgrims survive their first year at Plymouth. What was the name of these woodland people?

The **Wampanoags** showed the Pilgrims how to survive and plant native corn.

Colonial

In 1629 Puritans formed the Massachusetts Bay Company, which allowed them to settle on the land between the Charles and Merrimack rivers. Where did the Puritans settle?

a. Boston
b. New York
c. Plymouth
d. Jamestown

The Puritans settled at the mouth of the Charles River and established **Boston.** John Winthrop was elected as the first governor of the colony called the Massachusetts Bay Company. The colony was renamed Massachusetts in 1691. **(a)**

Colonial

In 1635 Lord Baltimore received a charter to start a new colony along Chesapeake Bay. To attract more people, land was granted to anyone who had what?

a. Lots of money
b. Servants, women, and children
c. The Catholic religion
d. A clean legal record

Unlike other colonies Lord Baltimore granted land to anyone who brought with them **servants, women, and children.** Lord Baltimore also passed an "Act of Toleration," which provided religious freedom to all Christians so long as they remained loyal to him and the government. **(b)**

AMERICAN HISTORY

AMERICAN HISTORY

AMERICAN HISTORY

AMERICAN HISTORY

AMERICAN HISTORY

AMERICAN HISTORY

AMERICAN HISTORY

AMERICAN HISTORY

AMERICAN HISTORY

Colonial

What was William Penn's original settlement in America called?

In 1681 King Charles II granted land in the middle colonies to William Penn, a Quaker. His settlement was called **Philadelphia** after the Greek words for "love," or "friendly" and "brother." Penn's colony was called Pensylvania, meaning Penn's woods.

Colonial

Name **two crops** commonly grown on plantations in the early- to mid-1700s?

Many plantations, or estates farmed by laborers, grew **tobacco, rice, and indigo** (a plant that is used to make blue dye). Tobacco had been a profitable crop since the early 1600s. It wasn't until Eli Whitney's cotton gin was in full use in the early 1800s that cotton became a major cash crop.

Colonial

Because the French built forts to protect their lands throughout New France, the English found little room to expand beyond the Appalachian Mountains. When the English tried to move into the Ohio River Valley claimed by the French, trouble brewed. What was the name of the war that unofficially started in 1754?

The **French and Indian War**, which officially began in 1756, got its name from the people the English were fighting. In 1754, it was George Washington who led an army into the Ohio Valley to push back the French at Fort Duquesne (now Pittsburgh).

Colonial

The English won the French and Indian War after capturing Quebec because the French could no longer supply their forts. With the war officially ended at the signing of the Treaty of Paris in 1763, what did the English win?

a. Louisiana
b. Rights to trade with the French
c. All of France's land
d. All of the above

In the Treaty of Paris, **Britain gained Canada and all the French lands east of the Mississippi River**. Spain, which had fought on the side of France, gave up **Florida** in exchange for what is now Cuba. **(c)**

Colonial

This boundary or fictitious line became commonly known as the dividing line between the free and slave states. It later divided the northern states from the southern states during the Civil War. What is the name of this line named after the two Englishmen who surveyed the boundary beginning in 1765?

The dividing line was between eastern Pennsylvania and western Maryland. The two men were Charles Mason and Jeremiah Dixon. The boundary became known as the **Mason-Dixon Line.**

Colonial

This grandson of a blacksmith grew up to be one of the most famous men in the colonies. He founded Philadelphia's first newspaper, public library, and hospital. Who was this man who published *Poor Richard's Almanac* and invented the lightening rod, bifocal eyeglasses, and the iron stove?

Philadelphia's industry grew with the help of **Benjamin Franklin.**

Colonial

New England ships carried fish and lumber to the West Indies in exchange for sugar and molasses. The sugar and molasses was brought back to the colonies to make rum. In turn, rum and guns were shipped to West Africa in exchange for slaves. Then, the slaves were sold in the West Indies in exchange for sugar and molasses, and so on. What was the name of this system of trade called?

Triangular trade.

Revolutionary War

In 1765 the British imposed the Stamp Act on colonists to cover the debts incurred by fighting the French and Indian War. The Stamp Act was a tax on which products?

a. Stamps and letters
b. Iron and glass products
c. Paper products and documents
d. Toys and games

Colonists had to pay taxes when they bought newspapers, almanacs, playing cards, and on legal documents like wills, diplomas, and marriage certificates (**paper products and documents**). The word *stamp* referred to the seal or stamp that was printed on the paper after the tax was paid. **(c)**

Revolutionary War

The colonists benefited from the outcome of the French and Indian War. Why were they upset over a tax the British Parliament passed to help pay for the war?

a. Because Parliament, made up of English representatives, passed the tax.
b. They would have paid taxes; they just didn't like how the British did it.
c. They did not want taxation without representation.
d. All of the above.

"No taxation without representation" is a phrase that dates back to 1215, when King John signed the Magna Carta—an agreement that stated the king would not govern or pass laws arbitrarily. **All of the above. (d)**

AMERICAN HISTORY

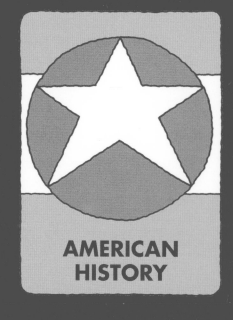

AMERICAN HISTORY

AMERICAN HISTORY

AMERICAN HISTORY

AMERICAN HISTORY

AMERICAN HISTORY

AMERICAN HISTORY

AMERICAN HISTORY

AMERICAN HISTORY

Revolutionary War

Groups of colonists who called themselves Sons of Liberty protested the Stamp Act of 1765. Parliament repealed the Stamp Act, but later passed acts that required colonists to pay taxes on imported items from England like tea, paper, glass, lead, and paint. What were these acts called?

a. Intolerable Acts
b. Townshend Acts
c. Acts of Duty
d. The Riot Acts

(b) Though the taxes were low, colonists still objected to being taxed without their interests being represented in English government. In an effort to get Parliament to repeal the **Townshend Acts**, colonists boycotted all products imported from England.

Revolutionary War

The first formal Committee of Correspondence was established in 1764. It was organized by a skilled lawyer, John Adams. Which statement is false?

a. The first committee of correspondence was formed in Boston.
b. The committee wrote letters and pamphlets about events.
c. The committees corresponded with other colonies.
d. The one colony that did not have a committee was Florida.

(d) Florida was not a colony and so it did not have a committee of correspondence.

Revolutionary War

When three ships carrying tea from England arrived in Boston Harbor, the captain was required to pay tax on the tea before unloading and selling it. What famous event took place on a November evening in 1773, when 50–60 colonists dressed as Mohawk Indians to dump 10,000 pounds of tea into the harbor?

The colonists dumped only tea into the harbor—no other cargo on the ships was touched. The effects from the **Boston Tea Party** were long lasting.

Revolutionary War

King George III of England believed Boston colonists should be punished for the Boston Tea Party. What did Parliament decide to do?

a. Close Boston Harbor
b. Refuse to buy American goods
c. Disown America
d. All of the above

(a) Parliament decided to **close Boston Harbor** until the colonists paid for the tea that was destroyed.

Revolutionary War

After the Boston Tea Party, Parliament passed several laws as punishment. Some of those laws limited colonists' town meetings to once a year and forced colonists to feed and house British soldiers. What did Colonists call Parliament's actions?

a. Incomprehensible Acts
b. Inexcusable Acts
c. Intolerable Acts
d. Instant Acts

(c) Colonists called these actions the **Intolerable Acts** because the laws were so harsh. With their port closed Bostonians lacked adequate food and supplies.

Revolutionary War

The First Continental Congress met in Philadelphia in 1774. What was the main reason for the meeting?

a. Discuss how to elect delegates
b. Discuss the colonist's response to the Intolerable Acts.
c. Draft the Declaration of Independence
d. All of the above

(b) The first Congress met to **discuss the colonies' response to the Intolerable Acts.** The colonists decided to boycott English goods and stop exporting to England until the harsh laws were repealed. They also urged each colony to set up its own militia (army).

Revolutionary War

True or false? Colonists who supported Britain during the Revolutionary War were often called Patriots?

False. Colonists who sided with Britain were called **Loyalists.** It was the colonists favoring independence who were often called Patriots.

Revolutionary War

On the night of April 18, 1775, this silversmith learned the British were leaving Boston to capture colonist weapons stored near Lexington and Concord. Rumor had it the British also planned to arrest two patriot leaders, Sam Adams and John Hancock. Who rode to Lexington to warn the two men?

William Dawes, a shoemaker, and Samuel Prescott, a doctor, joined **Paul Revere** on the ride that night. Henry Wadsworth Longfellow wrote in his 1863 poem about the event: "Listen my children and you shall hear of the midnight ride of Paul Revere."

Revolutionary War

In 1775 farmers, craftsmen, business owners, and wealthy men joined together to defend the towns and cities. These men were required to be ready for battle in very little time. What were those men called?

Because they kept their muskets at hand and were prepared to fight at a minute's notice they became known as **minutemen.**

AMERICAN
HISTORY

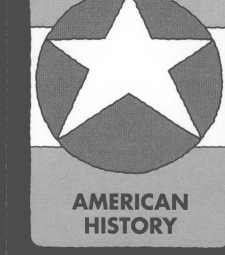

AMERICAN
HISTORY

AMERICAN
HISTORY

AMERICAN
HISTORY

AMERICAN
HISTORY

AMERICAN
HISTORY

AMERICAN
HISTORY

AMERICAN
HISTORY

AMERICAN
HISTORY

Revolutionary War

This Virginian often argued in favor of protecting colonial rights before the House of Burgesses. In March of 1775, he said "I know not what course others may take; but as for me, give me liberty or give me death." Who was this famous orator?

a. Robert E. Lee
b. Thomas Jefferson
c. Patrick Henry
d. Richard Henry Lee

Patrick Henry was well known for his speeches. He often encouraged colonists to protect their rights by fighting for their independence. **(c)**

Revolutionary War

The first armed battles between the minutemen and British took place in April of 1775 in what two towns?

The first armed clashes took place near the towns of **Lexington** and **Concord** in Massachusetts. Though no one knows who fired first, the shots were heard "round the world." This show of force by the colonists demonstrated to the British that the colonists were willing to fight for their rights.

Revolutionary War

The British had highly trained and experienced troops and a powerful navy, but it took months for them to receive news and supplies from England. What advantages did the untrained American troops have in the Revolutionary War?

a. They were fighting to defend their homes, shops, and farms.
b. They were fighting for their rights.
c. They owned rifles and were good shots.
d. All of the above.

All of the above. (d)

Revolutionary War

Why did colonists want to capture Fort Ticonderoga, which was located on Lake Champlain?

a. To use the fort as their hideout
b. To cut off British support from Canada
c. To aid the invasion of Canada
d. All of the above

The fort had many cannons, which the colonists needed to defend other areas from invasion. And having the fort would help colonists **cut off British support from Canada. (b)**

Revolutionary War

When the Second Continental Congress met in 1775, they nominated a Virginian to be Commander-in-Chief of the Continental Army. Who was this man?

George Washington, a soldier with extensive military training and experience, was nominated to head the first Continental Army.

Revolutionary War

The first major battle in the American Revolution was the Battle of Bunker Hill in 1775. If colonists secured Bunker Hill, they could fire upon British ships in Boston Harbor. Who won this first major battle?

Because the colonists were so low on ammunition, Colonel William Prescott is said to have told them, "Don't shoot until you see the whites in their eyes!" **The English** won Bunker Hill, but not before losing more than a thousand soldiers.

Revolutionary War

Two years after this talented English writer settled in Pennsylvania in 1774, he wrote an influential pamphlet entitled *Common Sense*. It used plain language and a plea to follow "common sense" in an effort to persuade colonists to form their own government. Who wrote this pamphlet?

a. Patrick Henry
b. Thomas Paine
c. Thomas Jefferson
d. George III

Thomas Paine wrote *Common Sense* in 1776. It documented his opinion that people have a natural right to their own government. George Washington said "I find *Common Sense* is working a powerful change in the minds of many men." **(b)**

Revolutionary War

When the Second Continental Congress sent him an Olive Branch Petition in an effort to make peace and ask him to repeal the Intolerable Acts, King George III called the colonists traitors. The king's refusal to repeal the acts inspired the colonists to form a committee and write a document. What did the colonists write?

John Hancock, the president of the Continental Congress, asked John Adams, Benjamin Franklin, Thomas Jefferson, Roger Sherman, and Robert Livingston to form a committee to write the **Declaration of Independence.**

Revolutionary War

What did the English offer slaves if the slaves helped the English soldiers fight the colonists?

a. Free passage to England
b. Freedom from slavery
c. Land for farming
d. Tea and silver

The British offered slaves **freedom. (b)**

AMERICAN HISTORY

AMERICAN HISTORY

AMERICAN HISTORY

AMERICAN HISTORY

AMERICAN HISTORY

AMERICAN HISTORY

AMERICAN HISTORY

AMERICAN HISTORY

AMERICAN HISTORY

Revolutionary War

The winter of 1776 was difficult for General Washington's troops. Thomas Paine wrote, "These are the times that try men's souls." To what was Paine referring?

a. The Continental army had extremely low morale.
b. It was difficult deciding whether to be a Loyalist or Patriot.
c. He and others lost family and friends.
d. None of the above.

Daily life for soldiers was enormously difficult and **morale was low**. Soldiers often fought without adequate food, shelter, and ammunition. **(a)**

Revolutionary War

The American victory at the Battle of Saratoga was a turning point in the Revolutionary War. Why?

a. It boosted American spirits.
b. It all but ended British threats to New England.
c. It helped convince France to become an ally.
d. All of the above.

All of the above are true. The turning point came when France was convinced the Patriots could win. They were still angry over losing the French and Indian War against the English and were now willing to help the colonists. **(d)**

Revolutionary War

British General Cornwallis's servant, James Armistead, spied on behalf of the Americans. Armistead gave Cornwallis false information, enabling George Washington's troops and the French to defeat British troops. Because the French navy kept English boats out of Chesapeake Bay, the English troops could not receive supplies or escape. They surrendered. What was the last major battle of the Revolution?

The Battle of Yorktown was the last major battle of the Revolution. Cornwallis had held out for three weeks before surrendering his army on Oct. 19, 1781. Cornwallis surrendered in full uniform to General Washington.

Early Nation

What was the name of the treaty that ended the Revolutionary War?

a. The Olive Branch
b. Treaty of Paris
c. Treaty of London
d. Treaty of Petitions

In the **Treaty of Paris** of 1783, England recognized the United States as an independent nation. The new borders extended from the Atlantic Ocean to the Mississippi River, from Canada south to Florida (but did not include Florida). Florida was given back to Spain for helping the colonists keep the English out of Louisiana. **(b)**

Early Nation

During the Revolution each of the colonies wrote a constitution to govern themselves. The colonies were rarely united. The Second Continental Congress in 1781 ratified what document to set up our country's central government?

a. The Bill of Rights
b. The Declaration of Independence
c. The Articles of Confederation
d. The Pledge of Allegiance

The Articles of Confederation, our country's first constitution, was ratified in 1781. **(c)**

Early Nation

Under the Articles of Confederation each state agreed to send one delegate for one vote in Congress. Which of the following were shortcomings to America's first constitution?

a. States printed their own money.
b. Most of the power was given to each state and not the Congress.
c. Congress could pass laws but not enforce them.
d. All of the above.

All of the above. Trade between states was difficult because each state used a different currency. With no central court system, disputes between states could not be settled. The Articles of Confederation formed an alliance between the states. **(d)**

Early Nation

During the war, demand for farm products was great. Farmers borrowed money for seed, tools, and land to produce more crops. And, after the war the nation suffered an economic depression. Massachusetts farmers rebelled when their taxes were raised. What was this rebellion called?

a. Shay's Rebellion
b. The Boston Massacre
c. The Farmer's Crisis
d. The Taxing Rebellion

Shay's Rebellion proved the Articles of Confederation were weak and ineffective. **(a)**

Early Nation

By 1787 the states knew the Articles of Confederation were ineffective. Delegates from each state met that summer to decide on a new course. Where did the 55 delegates meet and who was elected president of the Constitutional Convention?

They met in **Philadelphia** in 1787. **George Washington** was elected president of the Constitutional Convention.

Early Nation

In the early 1800s France was at war with England while America remained neutral, even though American ships were repeatedly attacked. Britain was thought to be giving Native Americans guns, causing anguish to colonial settlers in the west. Congress approved going to war with England. What did Congress name the war?

The War of 1812.

**AMERICAN
HISTORY**

**AMERICAN
HISTORY**

**AMERICAN
HISTORY**

**AMERICAN
HISTORY**

**AMERICAN
HISTORY**

**AMERICAN
HISTORY**

**AMERICAN
HISTORY**

**AMERICAN
HISTORY**

**AMERICAN
HISTORY**

Early Nation

Britain defeated France in 1814 and now had the resources to send ships and troops to fight America. Name two things Dolley Madison took with her when she was forced to leave the White House because the British were burning the capital?

She took with her **a portrait of George Washington, her parrot, and a copy of the Declaration of Independence.** All that was left of the President's home was the charred walls. Later the walls were painted white, inspiring the name the "White House."

Early Nation

During the War of 1812, the British captured a lawyer named Francis Scott Key. From where he was, he could see British cannons fire on Fort McHenry through the night. At dawn Key saw that the American flag was still flying above the fort. Inspired by the flag, what poem did he write that was later set to music?

Key wrote **"The Star Spangled Banner."** Later the poem was set to music and became America's official national anthem in 1931.

Early Nation

This invention improved production of cotton by deseeding it quickly. The invention in turn spurred continued slavery in the South as slaves grew and picked cotton, which brought profits to planters. Profits were then used to buy more land and slaves. What was this invention?

The invention that deseeded cotton quickly was the "cotton gin."

Early Nation

What did Congress pass in 1820 that balanced the number of free state and slave state representatives in the Senate?

a. The Louisiana Compromise
b. The Kansas Compromise
c. The Missouri Compromise
d. The Senatorial/Slavery Compromise

The Missouri Compromise created an imaginary line or boundary. To offset Missouri, a slave state, Maine was admitted to the Union as a free state. States below the Ohio River and east of the Mississippi River were designated as slave states. **(c)**

Early Nation

The Fugitive Slave Act of 1850 was part of the Compromise of 1850 laws. Henry Clay petitioned Congress to pass the laws. Who did the law benefit most—the North, South, neither or both?

The Fugitive Slave Act increased Northern opposition to slavery because they were required to capture and return runaway slaves. **The South benefited** by having the Northerners return slaves.

Early Nation

The Kansas–Nebraska Act **undid** the Missouri Compromise. It created the states of Kansas and Nebraska and allowed each state to elect whether it wanted slavery. What was the result of the Kansas election in 1855?

a. Kansas allowed slavery.
b. Kansas banned slavery.
c. Kansas both allowed and banned slavery.
d. The government decided for Kansas.

Two opposing sets of government were elected. **Kansas was in chaos. (c)**

Early Nation

In the 1850s people who opposed slavery were looking for a new political party. Their goal was to keep slavery out of the western territories. Abraham Lincoln was the first president that was from this party. What was the name of this new party?

Lincoln was the first president from the **Republican Party.**

Early Nation

In 1858 Abraham Lincoln said, "A house divided against itself cannot stand. I believe this government cannot endure permanently half slave and half free." What state was the first to secede from the Union?

In 1860 **South Carolina** voted to secede from the Union. Within two months Alabama, Florida, Georgia, Louisiana, Mississippi, Kansas, and Texas also seceded from the Union.

Civil War

After seven states seceded from the Union, a new nation formed. Those states called themselves the Confederate States of America. Who was the president of the Confederacy?

a. Andrew Jackson
b. Jefferson Davis
c. Robert E. Lee
d. William Sherman

The Declaration of Independence said the people have the right to alter or abolish the government if it denies the rights of citizens. Southerners thought Lincoln would deny them their assumed right to own slaves. **Jefferson Davis** became president of the Confederacy. Richmond became the capital. **(b)**

AMERICAN HISTORY

AMERICAN HISTORY

AMERICAN HISTORY

AMERICAN HISTORY

AMERICAN HISTORY

AMERICAN HISTORY

AMERICAN HISTORY

AMERICAN HISTORY

AMERICAN HISTORY

Civil War

After its formation, the Confederacy seized federal forts in the South. The opening shots of the Civil War were fired at which southern fort?

South Carolina's **Fort Sumter** guarded Charleston Harbor—an important position for the Confederates to hold.

Civil War

New technology made the Civil War more deadly. Rifles shot further. The Gatling machine gun could fire hundreds of shots per minute. Battleships were covered with iron in order to withstand powerful cannons. What are the reinforced battleships called?

These ships were called **ironclads.** Two well known ships were the Confederate's *Merrimack* and the Union's *Monitor.* Ironclads made wooden ships outdated, almost overnight.

Civil War

The industrialized North could provide its troops with supplies, ships, and rail transportation. The South had fewer resources. What kind of war did the South plan to fight?

a. Mainly defensive
b. Mainly offensive
c. A war that was fair
d. Any kind they could

Southerners were fewer in number, but were skilled horsemen and good shots. They were also defending their own farms and had the key advantage of fighting a **defensive war.** It was up to the North to attack and defeat the South. **(a)**

Civil War

The Civil War's first major land battle occurred in 1861 at a muddy stream called Bull Run. This battle was known by two names. Northerners primarily named battles after bodies of water while southerners named battles after land forms. What is the southern name for this battle and who won it?

Northerners called it the Battle of Bull Run. Southerners called it **the first Battle of Manassas. The South won.** People suddenly realized the rebellion might last a while.

Civil War

What is the name of the battle that finally enabled the Union to take control of the Mississippi River?

The Battle of Vicksburg.

Civil War

Two of the union's goals were achieved when General Ulysses S. Grant took control of the Mississippi River, dividing the South and preventing Southerners from trading with Europe. What battle occurred near a village on the Tennessee River and took the lives of thousands of men?

The number of casualties during the **Battle of Shiloh** was unprecedented on the American battlefield. The Battle of Shiloh occurred a few months before the Battle of Antietam.

Civil War

When President Lincoln issued the Emancipation Proclamation, people's views of the Civil War changed. How?

a. It was originally a war to preserve the Union, not to free slaves.
b. Southern slave owners were outraged.
c. With slavery an issue, it made it less likely that European countries would aid the South.
d. All of the above.

The Emancipation Proclamation changed the character of the war, which became an effort to unite the Union as well as an effort to end slavery. **All of the above. (d)**

Civil War

Union officials decided to get even with this man for siding with the south in the Civil War. They made his plantation in Arlington, Virginia, a burial ground for Union soldiers. This man commanded the Confederate Army and later surrendered to General Grant at the Appomattox Court House. Who was he?

General Robert E. Lee is the man whose former plantation is a national cemetery called Arlington Cemetery.

Civil War

Two victories in 1863 helped to change the course of the Civil War in favor of the North. The first one was at Vicksburg. What was the second battle called which was lead by Union General George Meade and Confederate General Robert E. Lee?

The Battle of Gettysburg was such a bloody battle the area was dedicated a few months later as a national cemetery by President Lincoln. There Lincoln gave an eloquent speech that lasted about three minutes, the Gettysburg Address.

AMERICAN HISTORY

AMERICAN HISTORY

AMERICAN HISTORY

AMERICAN HISTORY

AMERICAN HISTORY

AMERICAN HISTORY

AMERICAN HISTORY

AMERICAN HISTORY

AMERICAN HISTORY

Civil War

This Union General practiced Total War, destroying everything in his path that could be used by the South. He captured and burned Atlanta, then carved a path of destruction on his way to capture Savannah. Who was he?

a. General Lee
b. General Sheridan
c. General Sherman
d. General Grant

Grant, Sherman, and Sheridan practiced a type of war called Total War. But it was **Sherman who captured Atlanta and** Savannah. **(c)**

Civil War

After the South lost Richmond and Petersburg, General Ulysses S. Grant trapped the Confederates during the Appomattox campaign in Virginia. What was the name of the Confederate General whose surrender ended the Civil War?

General Robert E. Lee surrendered to Grant on April 9, 1865 at the Appomattox Court House. Lee told his troops he was proud of them and asked them to go home. Grant told the Union troops, "The war is over. The rebels are our countrymen now . . ."

Westward Expansion

New Orleans in the late 1700s was French, but American farmers used the port to export their goods. President Jefferson offered to buy it. Because France needed money to fight a war with England, they offered to sell it along with what is known as the Great Plains. What was this acquisition called? And, who later explored this territory?

In 1803, for $15 million the United States doubled in size when it bought this area in a deal known as **The Louisiana Purchase.** In 1804, Jefferson sent **Meriwether Lewis and William Clark** to explore the land. Their maps of the area helped settlers follow trails westward.

Westward Expansion

To aid travelers and freight haulers Congress approved spending to build a National Road from Cumberland, Maryland, through Virginia, Ohio, Indiana, and into Illinois. In what year did they begin construction of this National Road?

a. 1781
b. 1811
c. 1871
d. 1901

Work began in **1811.** By 1818 the road was completed to Wheeling, Virginia. Later the road was expanded into Illinois. Today it is known as Route 40. **(b)**

Westward Expansion

In the 1500s, the Spanish brought horses and cattle into present-day Texas. By the 1800s cowboys spent long days on cattle drives heading to railyards in Kansas, where cattle was often transported to meat packing plants in Chicago. What famous cattle trail's original path started in San Antonio and ran to Abilene, Kansas?

a. Santa Fe Trail
b. The Chisholm Trail
c. Oregon Trail
d. The Sedalia Trail

The **Chisholm Trail** ran from San Antonio into Abilene. When the railroad expanded into Texas, cattle drives came to an end. **(b)**

Westward Expansion

In 1830 steam locomotives were introduced in the United States. After that westward expansion became faster, easier, cheaper, and safer. What rail system was constructed to carry goods, animals, and people both east and west?

The Union Pacific and the Central Pacific constructed the **transcontinental railroad,** which allowed settlement westward to expand rapidly.

Westward Expansion

Plains Indians had used buffalo as one of their main sources of food and clothing, but by the late 1800s buffalo on the Plains had been drastically reduced in number. What caused the buffalo to disappear rapidly?

a. Longhorns
b. Railroads
c. Homesteaders
d. All of the above

Longhorn cattle competed with buffalo to eat the same prairie grasses. Railroads brought hunters who shot the buffalo for sport and money. To grow crops, homesteaders plowed under the grasses buffalo needed to survive. **All of the above. (d)**

Westward Expansion

Native Americans were not allowed to live in peace, even after they were forced to relocate to reservations in the late 1860s. Who was the colonel that tried to drive Native Americans out of the Black Hills of South Dakota after gold was discovered on a reservation?

At the Battle of Little Big Horn, two Lakota chiefs, Sitting Bull and Crazy Horse, fought and killed **Colonel George Custer** and his men. "Custer's last stand" was the Native Americans' last major victory on the Plains.

Westward Expansion

In 1867 what land, known as the "last frontier," was purchased? From whom was it purchased for $7.2 million dollars?

The land was purchased from Russia for $7.2 million dollars. The land later became known as the state of **Alaska.**

AMERICAN
HISTORY

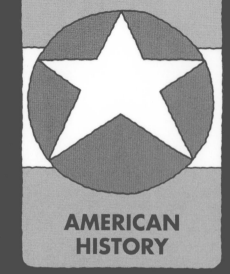

AMERICAN
HISTORY

AMERICAN
HISTORY

AMERICAN
HISTORY

AMERICAN
HISTORY

AMERICAN
HISTORY

AMERICAN
HISTORY

AMERICAN
HISTORY

AMERICAN
HISTORY

Westward Expansion

From the mid-1800s (until just before the Civil War) hundreds of thousands of people traveled westward along the Oregon Trail, California Trail, Mormon Trail, and Santa Fe Trail. Why did many of these people flock to Sutter's Mill, California, in 1849?

Sutter's Mill was a saw mill in the American River valley where James Marshall found gold in the river. This started a **gold rush**. Miners were called "**forty-niners**." The year 1849 was the year many came to seek their fortune.

Immigration

Even before Robert Fulton's steamboat, there was a need for a faster method to transport people and goods from New York to the Great Lakes. To accomplish this goal engineers hired farmers and then immigrants from Europe to construct what structure?

From 1817, the immense job of constructing the **Erie Canal** began. It was completed in 1825. The canal lowered the cost of shipping goods and helped make New York a center of commerce.

Immigration

What series of events, resulting from a natural disaster in Europe, led to tens of thousands of Irish to emigrate to the United States?

a. The Black Plague of Northern Europe
b. Asian Beetle Locust
c. Tsunamis in the Adriatic Sea
d. The Irish Potato Famine

Between 1846 and 1850, a fungus devastated crops and made the price of food skyrocket in Ireland. Many Irish starved to death. Others died from cholera and typhus. Hundreds of thousands of Irish tried to escape the **Irish Potato Famine** by emigrating to United States and other nations. **(d)**

Immigration

As the immigration rate increased in the mid-1800s, pressures to limit immigrant rights increased. Substantial political pressure came from the Know-Nothing Movement, named for organizations whose members wished to keep their identities and activities secret. What did proponents of this movement encourage?

a. Star-Spangled Bannerism
b. Nativism
c. Partisanship
d. Americanism

Advocates of **nativism** believed fundamental "American" views were in peril. The Order of United Americans and the Order of the Star-Spangled Banner were two of the most prominent organizations involved in the Know-Nothing Movement. **(b)**

Immigration

During the Gold Rush, fierce competition with Chinese immigrants for jobs helped lead to anti-Chinese sentiment. In response, Congress passed the Chinese Exclusion Act of 1882. What did this act do?

a. It banned the teaching of English to Chinese immigrants.
b. It forced Chinese immigrants to return to China.
c. It banned Chinese immigration.
d. It raised taxes on all goods made in China.

The Chinese Exclusion Act of 1882 banned **Chinese immigration** for a period of 10 years. **(c)** In 1892, the Geary Act extended the ban for 10 years. The Extension Act of 1904 made the ban permanent. With the Chinese Exclusion Repeal Act of 1943, Chinese were again allowed to enter the United States legally.

Immigration

Before 1855, how were immigrants processed?

a. There were no immigration records kept prior to 1855.
b. There were no immigrants prior to 1855.
c. Immigrants received their documentation by mail.
d. Ship captains gave a passenger list to the Collector of Customs.

The ship's captain **gave a passenger list to the destination port's Collector of Customs**. After completing any necessary customs transactions, an immigrant's processing was considered complete. **(d)**

Immigration

In 1862 President Lincoln signed the Homestead Act. This act gave 160 acres of land to homesteaders, which included many immigrants, who lived on and farmed the land for five years. Where was this land located?

a. The Appalachians
b. The Southwest
c. The Great Plains
d. All of the above

Many Americans didn't think they could farm the dry grasslands of the **Great Plains,** so the government issued the Homestead Act. This encouraged people to move to Kansas, Nebraska, and the Dakotas. Immigrants from France, Denmark, Norway, Sweden, Russia, and Germany took advantage of this opportunity. **(c)**

Immigration

In the period between 1820 and 1890, one area of the world sent more immigrants to the United States than any other. From where did more than 13 million people emigrate?

a. Africa
b. Europe
c. Asia
d. South America

More than 13 million **Europeans** came to the United States. They came for religious, political, economic, and other reasons. During that same period, less than two thousand Africans (not slaves) came to the United States as immigrants. **(b)**

Immigration

By the 1880s a great wave of emigration was underway. Millions of Eastern and Southern Europeans came to America, bringing with them their own languages, ideals, traditions, and ways of life. What did advocates of the Americanization movement want immigrants to do?

a. Assimilate
b. Accommodate
c. Cooperate
d. Commune

Fear that immigrants would not make efforts to **assimilate** or "fit in" to American society helped fuel the Americanization movement. **(a)**

AMERICAN HISTORY

AMERICAN HISTORY

AMERICAN HISTORY

AMERICAN HISTORY

AMERICAN HISTORY

AMERICAN HISTORY

AMERICAN HISTORY

AMERICAN HISTORY

AMERICAN HISTORY

Immigration

By the 1890s large numbers of immigrants were arriving in New York every day. Port officials decided to open a new processing station in 1892. What was the name of this new station where immigrants got off the boat?

....

Ellis Island, located in the New York Harbor, became a processing station for immigrants.

REWARD CARD

If you answer the next question correctly, you earn **500** points!
(If the 500 space has already been filled in for the category, answer a question from another category.)

REWARD CARD

If you answer the next question correctly, you earn **500** points!
(If the 500 space has already been filled in for the category, answer a question from another category.)

REWARD CARD

If you answer the next question correctly, you earn **DOUBLE** points!

REWARD CARD

If you answer the next question correctly, you earn **DOUBLE** points!

REWARD CARD

If you answer the next question correctly, you earn **TRIPLE** points!

REWARD CARD

If you answer the next question correctly, you earn **TRIPLE** points!

REWARD CARD

Save this card. If you answer a question incorrectly, turn this card in for a new question. Before losing any points, you have a **SECOND CHANCE** to score!

REWARD CARD

Save this card. If you answer a question incorrectly, turn this card in for a new question. Before losing any points, you have a **SECOND CHANCE** to score!

AMERICAN HISTORY

AMERICAN HISTORY

AMERICAN HISTORY

AMERICAN HISTORY

AMERICAN HISTORY

AMERICAN HISTORY

AMERICAN HISTORY

AMERICAN HISTORY

AMERICAN HISTORY

REWARD CARD

Save this card. If you need some extra help, turn this card in for a chance to **CHECK YOUR FACTS**! This card entitles you to consult with a resource before you answer.

REWARD CARD

Save this card. If you need some extra help, turn this card in for a chance to **CHECK YOUR FACTS**! This card entitles you to consult with a resource before you answer.

REWARD CARD

Save this card. If you need some extra help, turn this card in for a chance to **CHECK YOUR FACTS**! This card entitles you to consult with a resource before you answer.

The team who raises the first hand answers the next question. Good luck!

The team who raises the first hand answers the next question. Good luck!

The team who raises the first hand answers the next question. Good luck!

The team who raises the first hand answers the next question. Good luck!

PENALTY CARD

If you answer the next question incorrectly, subtract the point value from your score. Sorry!

PENALTY CARD

If you answer the next question incorrectly, subtract the point value from your score. Sorry!

AMERICAN
HISTORY

AMERICAN
HISTORY

AMERICAN
HISTORY

AMERICAN
HISTORY

AMERICAN
HISTORY

AMERICAN
HISTORY

AMERICAN
HISTORY

AMERICAN
HISTORY

AMERICAN
HISTORY